Cookii Cancer:

Nourishing Recipes for Managing Symptoms and Promoting Healing

Elizabeth O. Donald

Table of content

Introduction

If you or a loved one is living with cancer, you know that nutrition plays an important role in the fight against this disease. Proper nutrition can help boost the immune system, reduce inflammation, and provide the energy needed to take on cancer treatments. However, it can be challenging to know what to eat when you are dealing with the side effects of treatments like chemotherapy and radiation.

That's why we've created this cookbook, which is specifically designed for those living with cancer. Our recipes focus on nutrient-dense ingredients that not only taste delicious but also provide the body with the building blocks it needs to heal and fight cancer. This cookbook is also designed to be flexible, so whether you are going through a period of intense treatment or are in remission, there are recipes that will meet your changing needs.

How This Cookbook Can Help

Throughout this cookbook, you will find recipes that highlight whole grains, lean protein sources, and a variety of fruits and vegetables. We've also included flavorful recipes for those who may have lost their sense of taste or appetite due to treatments. Our hope is that this cookbook becomes a valuable resource for cancer patients, caregivers, and those looking to support a loved one through their cancer journey.

Chapter 1. Appetizers and Small Bites.

When undergoing cancer treatment, maintaining a nutritious and balanced diet is crucial to support the body's healing and recovery process. Including a variety of healthy snacks can help ensure an adequate intake of essential nutrients. Here are some snack ideas that can be beneficial for cancer patients:

A. High-Protein Snacks:

Protein is an essential nutrient for the body, as it helps in tissue repair and supports the immune system. Opt for high-protein snacks such as Greek yogurt, cottage cheese, hummus, nut butter (like almond or peanut butter), or protein bars. These snacks provide a good source of protein while also offering a range of flavors to suit different preferences.

B. Nutrient-Dense Dips and Spreads:

Dips and spreads can be a tasty and convenient way to incorporate nutrient-dense foods into your diet. Consider options like guacamole (made from avocado), salsa (made from tomatoes and other vegetables), or bean-based dips (such as black bean dip or white bean dip). These dips are rich in vitamins, minerals, and fiber, which can help support overall health.

C. Vegetable Skewers:

Vegetable skewers are a colorful and delicious snack that can provide important vitamins and antioxidants. Choose a variety of vegetables like cherry tomatoes, bell peppers, zucchini, mushrooms, or onions, and thread them onto skewers. You can enjoy them as is or grill them for added flavor. Vegetables are packed with essential nutrients and fiber, making them an excellent choice for cancer patients.

D. Chilled Soups:

During cancer treatment, you may experience side effects like mouth sores or a decreased appetite. Chilled soups can be a refreshing and soothing option that is easier to consume. Consider making soups using nutrient-rich ingredients like cucumber, avocado, spinach, or blended vegetable soups. These soups are not only hydrating but also provide a range of vitamins and minerals.

E. Baked Sweet Potato Fries:

Instead of traditional fries, baked sweet potato fries are a healthier alternative that offers a good source of dietary fiber, vitamins, and minerals. Slice sweet potatoes into thin strips, toss them with a little olive oil, and bake until they are crispy. They can be enjoyed as a satisfying snack and provide valuable nutrients that support overall well-being.

Chapter 2. Salads and Dressings

When it comes to supporting the health of cancer patients, incorporating nutrient-dense and flavorful salads into their diet can be beneficial. Salads are a great way to incorporate a variety of fruits, vegetables, and proteins that provide essential nutrients. Here are some salad ideas that can be helpful for cancer patients:

A. Dark Leafy Greens Salad:

Dark leafy greens like spinach, kale, or arugula are packed with vitamins, minerals, and antioxidants that can support overall health. Create a base with these greens and add toppings such as cherry tomatoes, cucumber slices, shredded carrots, and sliced bell peppers. You can also include a source of protein like grilled chicken, tofu, or chickpeas. Consider adding a sprinkle of seeds or nuts for an extra crunch and healthy fats.

B. Chopped Salad with Grilled Chicken:

Chopped salads are versatile and allow for a mix of colorful vegetables and proteins. Begin by chopping vegetables like romaine lettuce, cucumbers, cherry tomatoes, bell peppers, and red onions into bite-sized pieces. Add grilled chicken for a lean protein source. You can further enhance the flavor by including ingredients like feta cheese, olives, or avocado. Finish with a light dressing or vinaigrette to tie the flavors together.

C. Fruit and Nut Salad:

A fruit and nut salad is not only refreshing but also provides a variety of nutrients and flavors. Combine mixed greens with a selection of fruits such as berries, oranges, or diced apples. Incorporate some nuts or seeds like walnuts, almonds, or pumpkin seeds for added crunch and healthy fats. For a touch of sweetness, consider adding a drizzle of honey or a sprinkle of cinnamon. This salad offers a delightful blend of textures and tastes.

Making your own dressings allows you to control the ingredients and customize the flavors to your liking. Here are a few simple dressing recipes to try:

Lemon Vinaigrette: Whisk together fresh lemon juice, extra virgin olive oil, Dijon mustard, minced garlic, salt, and pepper. This light and tangy dressing complements a variety of salads.

Balsamic Vinaigrette: Mix balsamic vinegar, extra virgin olive oil, Dijon mustard, minced garlic, honey (optional), salt, and pepper. This versatile dressing adds a touch of sweetness and pairs well with a range of salad ingredients.

Yogurt Herb Dressing: Combine plain Greek yogurt, lemon juice, fresh herbs like dill or basil, minced garlic, salt, and pepper. This creamy dressing provides a tangy and herby flavor while adding a dose of protein.

Chapter 3.

Soups and Stews.

Bone broth-based soups have gained popularity in recent years due to their rich flavor and numerous health benefits. Made by simmering bones, such as beef or chicken, along with vegetables and herbs, bone broth is packed with essential nutrients, collagen, and gelatin. These soups are not only delicious but also provide nourishment to the body.

From classic chicken noodle soup to comforting beef and vegetable stew, bone broth-based soups offer a hearty and nutritious meal option.

B. Hearty Vegetable Stews:

Hearty vegetable stews are a fantastic choice for those looking to enjoy a satisfying and nutritious meal. Packed with an array of colorful vegetables, such as carrots, potatoes, celery, and bell peppers, these stews provide a hearty and comforting experience.

Vegetable stews are versatile and can be customized to include your favorite vegetables and spices. Whether you prefer a chunky tomato-based stew or a creamy vegetable medley, these dishes are a great way to incorporate more plant-based goodness into your diet.

Creamy cauliflower soup is a delightful option for those seeking a velvety and flavorful soup without the heaviness of cream-based soups. Cauliflower is the star ingredient in this dish, lending its mild and nutty flavor.

When blended with vegetable broth and seasoned with herbs and spices, cauliflower transforms into a creamy and satisfying soup. This soup is not only delicious but also low in calories and rich in vitamins and minerals. It serves as a great choice for individuals following a low-carb or plant-based diet.

D. Cold Gazpacho:

Cold gazpacho is a refreshing and vibrant soup that is perfect for hot summer days. Originating from Spain, this chilled soup is typically made with ripe tomatoes, cucumbers, bell peppers, onions, garlic, olive oil, and vinegar. Blended together, these ingredients create a tangy and refreshing soup that is served cold.

Cold gazpacho is not only a delicious way to beat the heat but also a great source of vitamins and antioxidants. Its light and zesty flavors make it a popular choice for those seeking a light and refreshing meal option.

Chapter 4.

Main Entrees.

Salmon is an excellent source of lean protein and omega-3 fatty acids, which have been shown to have anti-inflammatory properties and support heart health. Grilling salmon enhances its natural flavors while keeping it moist and tender.

Paired with asparagus, a nutrient-rich vegetable that provides fiber and essential vitamins, this dish offers a delicious and well-balanced meal for cancer patients.

Tuna is another protein-rich fish that can be seared to perfection and enjoyed alongside a colorful vegetable medley. Rich in antioxidants and fiber, the vegetable medley can include a variety of cancer-fighting vegetables like broccoli, bell peppers, carrots, and zucchini. This dish provides a satisfying and nutrient-dense option for cancer patients.

C. Baked Chicken with Root Vegetables:

Chicken is a lean source of protein that can be baked with a variety of root vegetables such as sweet potatoes, carrots, and parsnips. Root vegetables are packed with essential nutrients, including vitamins, minerals, and dietary fiber. Baking chicken and root vegetables together allows their flavors to meld, creating a comforting and nourishing meal option for cancer patients.

D. Beef Stew with Pearl Barley:

Beef stew with pearl barley is a hearty and nutritious option that can be prepared in a slow cooker or on the stovetop. Lean cuts of beef, combined with a variety of vegetables like carrots, celery, and onions, provide protein, vitamins, and minerals. Pearl barley, a whole grain, adds texture and fiber to the stew. This dish is not only flavorful but also a great source of energy for cancer patients.

E. Vegetarian and Vegan Entree Recipes:

For cancer patients following a vegetarian or vegan diet, there are numerous delicious and nutrient-dense options available. Plant-based proteins such as beans, lentils, tofu, and tempeh can be incorporated into meals like stir-fries, curries, grain bowls, and salads.

Including a variety of colorful vegetables, whole grains, and plant-based fats like avocado and nuts ensures a well-rounded and nourishing diet for cancer patients following a vegetarian or vegan lifestyle.

Chapter 5.

Sides and

Accompani

ments.

A. Roasted Vegetables:

Roasting vegetables is a simple and delicious way to bring out their natural flavors. Choose a variety of colorful vegetables like carrots, bell peppers, broccoli, and Brussels sprouts. Toss them with a little olive oil, sprinkle with herbs and spices, and roast until they are tender and slightly caramelized. Roasted vegetables are packed with vitamins, minerals, and fiber, making them an excellent addition to a cancer-friendly diet.

B. Quinoa and Brown Rice Pilafs:

Quinoa and brown rice are whole grains that provide a good source of fiber and essential nutrients. Prepare a flavorful pilaf by cooking quinoa and brown rice together with aromatic vegetables like onions, garlic, and bell peppers. Add herbs and spices such as turmeric, cumin, or parsley for added flavor. This dish offers a satisfying and nutritious side or main course option for cancer cooks.

C. Sweet Potato Mash:

Sweet potatoes are rich in vitamins A and C, fiber, and antioxidants. Create a creamy and comforting sweet potato mash by boiling or baking sweet potatoes until tender, then mashing them with a little olive oil, salt, and pepper. For added depth of flavor, consider incorporating spices like cinnamon, nutmeg, or paprika. Sweet potato mash is not only delicious but also provides important nutrients for cancer patients.

D. Vegan Caesar Salad:

A vegan Caesar salad can be a flavorful and refreshing addition to a cancer-friendly menu. Instead of traditional Caesar dressing made with anchovies and egg yolks, opt for a vegan version using ingredients like cashews, nutritional yeast, garlic, and lemon juice. Toss crisp romaine lettuce with the dressing and add toppings such as cherry tomatoes, croutons (preferably whole grain), and a sprinkle of vegan parmesan cheese. This salad is packed with vitamins, minerals, and antioxidants while offering a burst of flavors.

Chapter 6.

Desserts and Baked Goods.

A. Fruit Sorbets:

Fruit sorbets are a refreshing and guilt-free treat that can be made with a variety of fresh or frozen fruits. Simply blend the fruits of your choice, such as berries, mangoes, or citrus fruits, with a little lemon or lime juice and a natural sweetener like honey or agave syrup. Freeze the mixture until it reaches a sorbet-like consistency. These fruit sorbets are not only delicious but also provide vitamins, minerals, and antioxidants.

No bake cookies and bars are easy to make and require minimal effort. Using ingredients like oats, nut butter, seeds, dried fruits, and natural sweeteners, you can create a variety of delicious and nutrient-packed treats. Combine the ingredients, shape them into cookies or bars, and let them set in the refrigerator. These treats offer a satisfying texture and can be customized to suit individual preferences.

Healthy dessert bites are a fantastic option for portion-controlled indulgence. You can create a variety of bites using ingredients like dates, nuts, cocoa powder, coconut flakes, and spices. Simply blend or process the ingredients together, roll them into small balls or squares, and refrigerate until firm. These dessert bites offer a combination of flavors and textures while providing important nutrients like fiber, healthy fats, and antioxidants.

For cancer cooks who have dietary restrictions such as gluten-free or vegan, there are plenty of delicious options available. Experiment with gluten-free flours such as almond flour, coconut flour, or gluten-free oat flour to create cakes, muffins, and cookies. Utilize plant-based substitutes like applesauce, flaxseed meal, or mashed bananas in place of eggs. These baked goods can be enjoyed without worrying about ingredients that may trigger sensitivities or dietary restrictions.

Chapter 7.

Drinks and Smoothies.

A. Detox Smoothies:

Detox smoothies are a great way to incorporate a variety of fruits and vegetables into the diet, providing essential vitamins, minerals, and antioxidants. Blend together ingredients like leafy greens (such as spinach or kale), berries, citrus fruits, and a liquid base like almond milk or coconut water. These smoothies are not only delicious but also help to hydrate the body and support its natural detoxification processes.

B. Herbal Teas:

Herbal teas offer a soothing and comforting beverage option for cancer patients. Choose herbal teas such as chamomile, peppermint, ginger, or green tea, which are known for their calming and digestive properties. These teas can be enjoyed hot or iced and provide a hydrating and flavorful alternative to sugary or caffeinated drinks.

Cancer patients may want to enjoy a celebratory or social drink on occasion. Opt for healthy cocktails and mocktails that are low in added sugars and alcohol, focusing on fresh ingredients. For example, a mocktail could be made with sparkling water, muddled berries, a splash of citrus juice, and garnished with herbs.

Alternatively, a healthy cocktail might incorporate fresh herbs, such as basil or mint, with a splash of vodka or gin, combined with soda water and a squeeze of citrus. These options provide a refreshing and flavorful experience while keeping overall health in mind.

Chapter 8.
Resources.

When it comes to cancer and nutrition, having access to reliable resources is essential for making informed decisions about your diet and overall well-being. Here are some valuable resources for cancer patients:

American Cancer Society (ACS): The ACS provides comprehensive information on nutrition and cancer, including guidelines, recommendations, and resources to help patients and their caregivers make informed choices about their diet. Their website offers articles, recipes, and tips for managing nutrition during treatment and recovery.

National Cancer Institute (NCI): The NCI is a reliable source of evidence-based information on cancer prevention, treatment, and survivorship. Their website features resources on nutrition and cancer, including guidelines, research updates, and educational materials to help individuals make informed decisions about their dietary choices.

Oncology Nutrition Dietetic Practice Group (ON DPG): This specialized group of registered dietitians focuses on nutrition for individuals with cancer. Their website provides resources, articles, and tools to help cancer patients and healthcare professionals navigate nutrition-related issues during treatment and beyond.

Cancer Research UK: Cancer Research UK offers evidence-based information and resources on nutrition and cancer, including practical advice, recipes, and guidance for maintaining a healthy diet during and after cancer treatment.

Local Support Groups and Cancer Centers: Local support groups and cancer centers often provide resources, workshops, and educational materials on nutrition and cancer. Connecting with these organizations can provide personalized support and

access to additional resources specific
to your location.

Understanding the nutritional value and potential benefits of different ingredients is crucial for making informed choices when planning meals for cancer patients. Here's a glossary of common ingredients and their potential benefits:

Antioxidant-rich foods: Examples include berries, dark leafy greens, tomatoes, and nuts. These foods contain antioxidants that help protect cells from damage caused by free radicals.

Omega-3 fatty acids: Found in fatty fish (salmon, mackerel, sardines), flaxseeds, chia seeds, and walnuts, omega-3 fatty acids have anti-inflammatory properties and may support heart health and overall well-being.

Cruciferous vegetables: Vegetables like broccoli, cauliflower, Brussels sprouts, and kale are rich in phytochemicals and fiber, which have been associated with cancer-fighting properties.

Whole grains: Include whole grains like quinoa, brown rice, oats, and whole wheat bread in the diet. These provide fiber, vitamins, minerals, and sustained energy.

Plant-based proteins: Incorporate legumes (beans, lentils), tofu, tempeh, and edamame for plant-based protein sources that are also rich in fiber and other nutrients.

Healthy fats: Avocados, olive oil, nuts, and seeds are examples of healthy fats that can provide essential fatty acids and support overall health.

Herbs and spices: Herbs and spices like turmeric, ginger, garlic, and cinnamon offer potential health benefits such as anti-inflammatory properties and immune support.

CONCLUSION

As you come to the end of this journey through Cooking for Cancer, I hope you have found inspiration and practical guidance that will help you or your loved ones navigate the challenges of cancer treatment. Cooking for Cancer is more than just a collection of recipes - it's a way of thinking about food that can help you nourish the body, uplift the spirit, and create memorable moments with family and friends. Whether you are a seasoned cook or a beginner in the kitchen, I believe you will find joy and comfort in the power of food to heal and to inspire. May this book serve as a helpful guide and a source of hope as you continue on your journey toward recovery and wellness. Thank you for joining me on this culinary adventure, and may blessings and good health be yours always.

Printed in Great Britain
by Amazon

24586829R00030